How I Made Over
$1 Million
Using the Law of Attraction

How I Made Over $1 Million Using the Law of Attraction:

The Last Law of Attraction, How-To, or Self-Help Book You Will Ever Need to Read

E.K. Santo

Copyright

How I Made Over $1 Million Using the Law of Attraction:
The Last Law of Attraction, How-To, or Self-Help Book
You Will Ever Need to Read

By
Copyright 2012 by E.K. Santo

No part of this book may be reproduced without written consent.

eksanto.com
eksanto1966@gmail.com

Dedication

This book is dedicated to my wonderful wife, Concetta, and my two great children, Michael and Cristina. Without their love and support none of this would have happened.

Contents

Author's Foreword
Chapter One: My Journey
Chapter Two:
- The Law of Attraction and Creation
- Thoughts Become Things

Chapter Three:
- Vibration and Being
- How You Really Feel

Chapter Four:
- Desire
- Burning Desire

Chapter Five:
- Belief
- Faith and Trust

Chapter Six:
- Allowing and Receiving
- Gratitude is the Key

Chapter Seven:
- Inner Speech – How you Speak to Yourself
- Affirmations and Questions
- Positive Affirmations
- Empowering Questions

Chapter Eight:
- The Imagination
- Using Visualization Techniques to Create

Contents Continued-

Chapter Nine:
- More Information – Tips, Pointers and Other Help
- The Universe, Source Energy, Creation, Infinite Intelligence, God
- The Flow of the Universe
- Resistance
- Clearing
- Meditation
- Goals and Goal Setting – Your Purpose
- Love

Law of Attraction Cheat Sheet
Final Note
Resources
One Last Thing

Authors Foreword

Most people don't believe that they have control over their own lives. They go through life reacting to circumstances not realizing that they are the cause of these circumstances. I used to be one of those people, but I changed. This book is being written for you so that you may also change, if you so choose.

Yes it's another How-To book. Another Self-Help book. Another Law of Attraction book. This book in particular is making a really big claim...You can make $1,000,000 or more!

I know what you're thinking.

This guy has got to be kidding!

But the book isn't just about making a lot of money. It's about truly changing your life.

Aren't you tired of seeing another *NEW* book or program on the subject of the Law of Attraction, claiming they have the hidden, unknown secret to wealth, health, and happiness? Or better yet the ones that tout they have the *NEW* or *Better* method to make the Law of Attraction work for you!

COME ON!

The reality of naming this book "How I Made Over $1 Million Using the Law of Attraction: The Last Law of Attraction, How-To, or Self-Help Book You'll Ever Need to Read" is threefold.

1. I needed to get your attention!
2. I want you to know IT IS POSSIBLE! I know this because this stuff worked for me! I decided to pass it on to people who need the help.
3. This is not *'new'* or *'better'*, or some *'unknown secret'*.

Simply put, this book puts together the basics and the *'how-tos'* of the Law of Attraction and Self Improvement in a simple and clear, no-nonsense way. This book is for people who are both novice and experienced when dealing with creating what they want in their lives. More specifically, the idea behind the book was for the people out there who buy more than one book on the subject. Even more specifically, it's for the folks who buy multiple books, and then CD programs, attend seminars, workshops...The folks who keep looking for that *Something*...The *Hidden Treasure*...The *Holy Grail*. The never-ending quest.

I, too, was one of those seekers.

However I had a wakeup call one day. One of my *Aha!* moments.

To be perfectly straightforward, I've read dozens of Law of Attraction books, dozens of self-help books, listened to hundreds of CD's, attended seminars, workshops, etc. I literally immersed myself in self-help and the law of attraction.

And you know what?

The stuff works when properly applied! But I realized (my Aha! moment) two very important things.

1. There were a lot of people not getting the results they were promised, and
2. That I didn't need all the books, CD's, and seminars. Believe me they were great and very inspiring, but totally unnecessary. I really only needed 2 or 3 books. THAT'S IT!

You see I realized, finally, that all this material on the subject, and all the authors and purveyors were selling the same exact thing! Oh yes the words may be a bit different from book to book, and one author may write with more flair than the other, but the techniques for using the Law of Attraction and manifesting all of your desires into reality are virtually the same!

"Think and Grow Rich" by Napoleon Hill..."The Science of Getting Rich" by Wallace D. Wattles..."The Master Key System" by Charles Haanel..."The Secret" by Rhonda Byrne... numerous titles by Jerry and Esther Hicks (the Abraham books)...Anthony Robbins,

T. Harv Ecker, Jack Canfield, Dr. Joe Vitale, Dr. Wayne Dyer...The list goes on and on.

I have read them all...And I come to you now with 3 conclusions...

1. They are all excellent, inspirational, and helpful. I'm in no way putting them down.
2. The information contained in the books works, if used and applied correctly.
3. They all basically say the exact same thing!

The point is this...If you've read more than one of the books by just the authors listed above; that's all you need. My guess is that you haven't put into practice the techniques these people promote to create the great life that you deserve.

If I bought and read 1 book, then another, and then another, and they all spell out to do the same thing...The simple answer is...**DO EXACTLY** what they say, with unwavering faith, and it will work! Instead most people (myself included) continue the *Holy Grail* search.

This is the time to stop! RIGHT NOW!

Let me show you from my own personal experience and knowledge how I made this work for me!
This is not new material!
There is no new material!
Stop searching for new material that doesn't exist!

What has been working for a select few for decades still works, and will continue to work. *There is no secret. There are no magical words. There is no mystical meditation.* Everything you ever needed to learn to be successful, wealthy, happy, healthy, and abundant was in the first book you read. And the third, and the seventh, and the ninety ninth book.

You **CHOSE NOT** to follow the instructions. You thought you needed more information. Why? My guess would be some form of resistance. Maybe fear. Maybe doubt. Maybe you felt it was just too good to be true.

You know what?

It is true!!

I want to help you. I've had a great deal of success with this stuff. Use this little book...A compilation of very down-to-earth principles, explanations, and exercises, that if followed will help you make all of your dreams come true once and for all!

Just take a leap of faith and promise YOURSELF one thing:

"THIS IS THE LAST BOOK I WILL EVER NEED TO READ ABOUT USING THE LAW OF ATTRACTION, TO CREATE THE LIFE I TRULY DESIRE!"

E.K. Santo

Chapter One

My Journey

I feel it is only fitting for you to know a bit about me and how I arrived here. My successes and failures (I don't consider there to be any failures actually, just learning experiences and obstacles) with self-help, the Law of Attraction and Creation, and personal achievement. Read this chapter once. It's not a part of the book that you'll need for future reference. I'm just impressing upon you that if you practice what is preached in this material, it can really work well.

To start, up until my early twenties I led a pretty average life. High school, girlfriends, cars. Nothing crazy. After I left high school I chose not to go to college, but opted for work. I had a few jobs, nothing to write home about. I recall working in a boring warehouse job as an assistant manager and living at home with Mom and Dad. I had no real prospects other than that I really loved the *prospect* of being wealthy. I had a real passionate desire to be rich, but not a clue how to do it. I also didn't think college was the answer. But I had a little ambition.

But a real *surge* of ambition came when I was watching television one night. I came across an infomercial about getting rich in the Real Estate business. I became excited, watching the fella on TV (I think it was Carleton Sheets) talking about buying property with 'No-Money Down', building up a Real Estate empire, and becoming rich.

So I ordered his program.

And then I went to the library and read books on real estate. I bought tape programs, went to seminars, and even became a part-time Real Estate agent. I completely immersed myself in the prospect of being the next Donald Trump!

I didn't buy any real estate.
I made one very small sale as an agent.
I didn't make any real money.

But two things did happen:

1. In my search for real estate knowledge, I came upon one program (infomercial) that definitely put me on the path to self-help, and then the Law of Attraction. It was Anthony Robbins "Personal Power" program. This was the first of many.
2. While still selling real estate as an agent, I met a customer interested in buying a multimillion dollar home. He was young, roughly my age, and very well to do. He also, like myself, never went to college, but earned a 7 figure income from his profession, a stockbroker. He was very impressed with my demeanor and salesmanship. This gentleman recommended that I should be a stockbroker!

How could I be a stockbroker? I knew nothing about the stock market. Nothing!

Well after listening to Tony Robbins tapes...About 10 times in a row, I became so inspired I decided to give it a shot!

Let me take a short break in my story and take a step back to see what had occurred. I had a dead end job, but did have an immense passion for becoming wealthy. The Universe (my word for the Creator of all things), in all its complex ways, gave me, step by step, what I asked for. I asked to be 'rich' in as simplistic a way as possible. I just didn't know it at the time. I hadn't become wealthy yet, but ideas, inspirations, people I kept meeting, and coincidences...All fell into place one after the other. If I had a better knowledge of the Law of Attraction/Creation (my way of thinking...it is creation) back then, I would have been able to create exactly what I wanted. I lacked clarity. I had no specific way of getting rich. But I was getting what I needed to become wealthy. The

Universe supplied me with every circumstance necessary to get to my end result.

Back to my story:

So I started my stockbroker career. From 1993 to 1999, I did everything I could to be successful!

How much money did I make?

Very little.

It turned out after just 6 months of intense training that I really hated it. Really long hours...Pounding the phones trying to get people to buy stocks...The constant rejection...It was tough! And above all else, never really making people any money (this was my biggest obstacle about the business, but would eventually lead me to another AHA! moment.) So why didn't I give up? Well the biggest reason was because I was surrounded by other young guys making 6 figure paychecks...A Month!! I had to keep trying.

So after some time went by and with intense persistence, I began to have a little bit of success; and by little I mean tiny. But I kept at it, working hard, all the while listening to my Anthony Robbins "Personal Power" tapes over and over. I constantly listened, but I never practiced his instructions. I guess they motivated and inspired me, but I didn't take the time to do what he said.

Anyway, I didn't realize it then, but if you really hate what you're doing for a job or career, you probably won't prosper at it. That's Tony Robbins 101. So out of his whole program, I used one simple technique that turned everything around for me. But not in the way I expected.

Tony Robbins iterates in his program, "When you ask the Universe for something, be specific. Ask a better question!"

I had been asking myself: "How can I make money doing something I hate?" I changed this to: "How can I become wealthy from my career, and enjoy the process?"

What a difference that was! Every time I struggled in my career from that moment, I now always asked myself that question, not really *knowing* the answer, but kind of expecting one. Hoping with very positive expectation. And I got what I asked for, but again, not exactly what I expected. I say this for a second time because I *thought* I would be successful as a stockbroker, but that ended up being just a 6 year pit-stop on the path to success.

One morning while just starting my day in the office, a new stockbroker showed up for work sitting at the desk next to me. He was very well groomed and dressed, looking like the epitome of success and wealth. We introduced ourselves, and then settled into work. I started my day on the phone prospecting for new clients as did all the other brokers in the office.

But he did something different.

He sat at his desk and studied a newspaper. After almost an hour, he picked up the phone and started calling his clients, one after the other with extreme enthusiasm...Telling each one that he found a really great growth opportunity, and they might make a lot of money if they invested in it.

He did this for quite a while. Talking into the phone, writing up buy tickets, calling the orders into the trading desk...Making Commissions!! By the time the day had ended he easily racked up at least $10,000 in commissions!

I was intrigued.

He read the paper. Dialed the phone. Made money! I never saw a broker do it quite like this.

I was taught to prospect for clients. Once you had a reasonable amount of clients, convince them, through the hard sell, to buy a firm-recommended stock.

And just keep doing that. Unfortunately, the firm's recommended stocks rarely worked out, so it was tough to keep a good client/broker relationship. But that's another story.

Before this money machine of a broker left for the day, he looked over at me and said, "If you want to make your clients some money, don't buy the 'house' stocks...Check this stock out. I think it should do well."

With that being said, he threw his newspaper on my desk and left. The newspaper had notes and highlights all over it from the new guy. The newspaper, which I had never seen before, was called "Investors Business Daily".

Believe it or not, this moment changed my life forever!

In a nutshell, this newspaper was written to aid the investor or trader in picking stocks, unlike the "Wall Street Journal" or "Barron's", both of which print yesterday's business news.

I sat for hours reading this *stock picking* newspaper. When I finished I had a brainstorm...I would become an amazing stock picker. "How easy it would be to make people money" I thought.

"And commissions for myself!"

I spent the next several weeks and months reading everything I could find about picking stocks, chart reading, company fundamentals, etc. You would think a brokerage firm would teach new stockbrokers this stuff, but they only teach salesmanship.

"You can't buy stocks without clients" they would say. I agreed with needing clients, but let's try to make them money, no? The firm's take was "If the firm makes money, and the broker makes money, but the client loses money...That's 2 out of 3, which ain't bad".

So they didn't care.

But I did.

It was at this time that I **'accidentally'** found my first Law of Attraction book. Even though Tony Robbins makes brief mentions of the Law of Attraction, his program was geared to something called Neuro-Linguistic Programming (NLP for short). It deals primarily with neurological processes, language, and behavioral patterns that have been learned through experience. It's an excellent program, and I still recommend it to people to this day, even though it has aged.

Anyway, the first Law of Attraction book I found was Napoleon Hill's "Think And Grow Rich", which Tony Robbins mentioned in his program as a must read book. I accidentally came upon the book at the bookstore while I was looking for a *how to get rich in the stock market* type of book.

The book completely intrigued me, especially the parts which mention *coincidences* happening at just the right time. It explained how to use your mind to create wealth, health, happiness, or any other endeavor; but really focusing on becoming rich. You can and will do more for mankind if you're wealthy versus being poor. I bought the book, and also made a decision...To find out more about this *creating process* while continuing to learn more and more about the stock market.

At this juncture I still wasn't making much money as a stockbroker, but I knew, like I've never known before, that this was all leading to big things. I could just feel it! But it wasn't going to turn out the way I had thought...The Universe had bigger and better plans than I did.

As the months ticked by I started to feel confident in my stock picking ability, so I began to (attempted to) get new clients to buy my stock picks. The thing was, I couldn't really get anyone to buy. Once in a while I got a 'yes', but it was mostly 'no'. I felt like I was failing (remember there is no failing, only learning experiences!)
Was all this stuff...BULLS**T? CRAP? HOGWASH?
I was really frustrated. What was I missing?
I took a deep breath. I remembered my Tony Robbins 101...I asked a better question. Actually the original question: "How can I become wealthy in my career, and enjoy the process?" But I didn't just ask myself once or twice...I began asking it of myself all day long, like an affirmation; a new technique I picked up from "Think and Grow Rich". I also treated this book the same way I treated Tony Robbins program; just taking a tidbit or two of information, and using just that. Not really practicing the instructions to the fullest. But between asking the right question, and focusing on it with very powerful *belief*, things started happening.
Belief...Having faith is by far the most important quality to create your future, and this was heavily noted in "Think and Grow Rich".
Within one week of my doing this new *'ritual'*, two very notable coincidences happened:

1. Another Law of Attraction book fell in my lap: "The Science of Getting Rich", by Wallace D. Wattles, and
2. A small IRA retirement account which I had started at an old job also popped up. I hadn't realized that I had access to it until I ran into an old friend from the old job, and we got to talking. He mentioned that the workers had more control over their retirement funds. A light bulb

went off in my head! "Did I have any money in my IRA? I completely forgot about it!" One phone call later and I was $3000 richer! I know it's not much, but it was just enough to put me in a position where I could start buying and selling stocks for myself.

Firstly, I took to the "Science of Getting Rich" like a fish to water. The book reads similarly to "Think and Grow Rich", but much simpler. I really absorbed the simple, yet powerful system, not realizing yet that this was the Law of Attraction in action.

Secondly, I started trading stocks in my little account. After just 3 months of trading the account, which started at $3000.00, I six-folded my money to $18,000! I finally found my passion and true calling! I was really excited!

Unfortunately there were still a few hiccups along the way, and I'll breeze through the next few years (yes years) quickly.

Now even though I worked in a brokerage firm, the management frowned upon trading stocks for my own account. They wanted commissions. They also didn't love the fact that many brokers in the office were using my stock picks to give to their clients instead of the firm's picks.

So, I had to leave that firm, go to another brokerage firm, and set up my trading account, all the while making it seem that I was an up-and-coming stockbroker. The fact was...I couldn't 'sell' fish to a hungry Eskimo. But I knew how to pick stocks and trade.

Over the next few years I would have to do this at three more brokerage firms, all the while trading when I could, and living off my profits. But because I needed the trading profits I was making to survive, I couldn't build my account up to anything substantial in value.

So in 1998 I made a decision; a tough one...I decided to leave the brokerage business and trade full time. In order to do that, my wife and I sold our condo, and moved into a small basement apartment in her parent's home. There was an extra room in the apartment. I set up a small office to trade stocks. With the sale of the condo, I now had about $40,000.00 to trade with. That was it. Our life savings.

I began what I considered to be my dream job. In the beginning it went well, but I soon realized the trading account still did not have enough money in it for me to become wealthy. I was making money, but just enough to get by on. Since I always had to take money out to live the account just couldn't grow. I felt I was so close to my dream, yet there always seemed to be one obstacle after another popping up. What should I do? What was I missing?

And once again, I took a step back...Ask a better question, and you'll receive a better answer. "How can I become a really successful trader, and enjoy the process?"

I phrased that question to myself morning, noon, and night. And for the first time I had a true inspiration that popped into my head one night right before bed. "Maybe the answer to my question was in one of my 2 books, "The Science of Getting Rich" or "Think and Grow Rich."

I'd read both of these books and became inspired, but never followed the instructions in the books to the letter. I guess you could say I used them 'half-assed'.

I decided, for no particular reason, to immerse myself in "Think and Grow Rich". Instead of just reading it, I absorbed it, inhaled it, and lived it. I followed its instructions exactly as the author recommended. And as stated in the book, an unexpected, but inspiring coincidence occurred.

A new trading book had just been published, and I was dying to go buy it. So on a Saturday afternoon I found myself in the bookstore, once again looking for another stock book (I currently own over 100 titles). After I found the trading book, I started to casually walk around the store. I found myself in the personal development section, when an author's name on the binding of a book suddenly stood out at me. Shakti Gawain. I thought to myself "What a funny name!", and grabbed the book called "Creative Visualization". I skimmed it, and read the back cover. I suddenly became very excited. This seemed to be exactly what I needed. I purchased both books.

What I started applying from "Creative Visualization", combined with the similar knowledge from "Think and Grow Rich", moved me forward so quickly, and unexpectedly, I'm shocked even to this day.

The basic premise is to use visualization, or your imagination, to produce results. You use the imagination to the point that you're already living your desires; sort of like fast-forwarding your life to where you want it to be or you already have a specific object that you desire. The book was written in such plain English that it was easy to master. I realized that this subject was written about in "Think and Grow Rich", but the language was so old and cumbersome I hadn't realized what Napoleon Hill was talking about. Also, this was the first book I had read that really spoke fluently of the Law of Attraction.

Author's Note
It was after I bought this book that I began continuously buying books, CD's, and other programs of it's like because I had great success with the techniques the author wrote about. I felt there had to be more great info out there. But to be completely honest with you, and myself, the 3 books were all I needed!

So I began to visualize (use my imagination) that I was this incredible trader. I was already amazingly wealthy. I had my dream home. Cars. Luxury vacations. You name it. I used this visualization technique right before bed, and just after awakening. The key though, was to stick to the end results of my desires with complete, unwavering FAITH, which I chose to do...No Matter What!

After a week or so, the Universe played a *'trick'* on me. You see the toughest part about using the Law of Attraction and having total belief and faith in your outcome is that we try to *control* events and circumstances to accomplish our goals. We try to control the path, the method, everything...to reaching our desires. But sometimes (more than sometimes), the Universe has a better way. It may not seem it at the time, but it always ends up like this. (In an upcoming chapter I'll get deeper into detail about setting your desires, and just going with the flow of the Universe.)

Anyway, I had this *vision* of how I wanted things to be, and I meditated on it daily. A week or so into it, my wife came home from a doctor's appointment. She informed me she was pregnant, and I would have to get a "Real Job", and give up this "Dream" of trading. Now most people get pretty excited about having a baby, and a part of me definitely was. But there was another part of me that felt like I just fell into a deep pit with no shovel or ladder.

I didn't get it! Maybe I was wrong, and this stuff doesn't really work! I was pissed off!

My wife saw my mixed emotions, and started to cry. This brought my emotions back into check, and I consoled her. I told her how happy I was, and that she just caught me off guard. I told her I would do whatever was necessary for our family.

How? I had no idea!

So at first I thought I should give up my dream; maybe go back to being a stockbroker or some similar job. I wasn't mad. I wasn't sad. Just resigned.

I recall this news came on a Tuesday, so I decided to look in the 'Help Wanted' ads in the upcoming Sunday newspaper. Over the next five days I continued with my visualization techniques. I *chose* to NOT give up. On Sunday I went out and got the newspaper. I opened to the 'Help Wanted' section. Plenty of stockbroker help wanted ads, insurance and mutual fund sales, and TRADERS WANTED…

What??!!

There were about 10 'Help Wanted' ads looking for traders. I was totally floored. I never even knew that trading firms existed. The exuberance that I went through at that moment was beyond belief. Happiness, confusion, relief, excitement…POSSIBILITY!

As it just so happened, a trading firm had opened a new office only a 15 minute drive from where I lived, and they were looking for experienced traders, but also open to newbies. What a coincidence! I thought I fell somewhere in-between expert and novice. I called for an interview, and you can guess how it went.

They made me an offer. A 6 month trial period, the first 3 months I would be learning and showing them what skills I had. If the first 3 months went well, the following 3 months I would be offered a 'draw' of $1000.00 per week ($50,000 per year), drawn against a 40% payout in profits using the firms money. I was a bit nervous about not earning a nickel for the first 3 months, but they didn't ask for any of my own money to put in the account. I chose to just let go of that bit of fear.

In my eyes this was a great opportunity. I still desired to trade on my own terms, and really would have preferred working from home and doing my own thing, but I couldn't pass this up.

After 3 months the firm's management was pretty impressed, and I moved on to my next 3 month trial period. I traded small shares, learned quite a bit from the other traders who sat around me in the office, and was getting a small salary to boot.

The 3 month trial whizzed by, and I continued to prosper. In December 1999 I was finished with my trial period. I had done well, and was now allowed to 'put the pedal to the metal'! And I did!

That December my gross profit was a bit over $48,000.00!

I went on over the next 11 years never having a losing week...EVER! I have averaged a steady 6 figure income and some 5-6 figure bonuses as well.

On top of that, due to the advancements in technology over the years I've been able to spend the last 6 years working from home. I literally trade the markets in my pajamas! Earning a six figure income!

The path to my desires was never straight. It always twisted and turned. The outcome however, was more amazing than I had anticipated.

Now I mentioned that the Universe may have a few *'tricks'* up its sleeve. I thought that my wife coming home pregnant and stating I needed to go get a job was the end of my dream. But I had so much faith to realizing my desires, it turned out that it was a *'necessary'* event to get me to my desire. If we hadn't become pregnant, my wife wouldn't have told me to get a "Real Job", and I would never have looked in the 'Help Wanted' ads for a job, and so on.

I chose to see it as a *bad* event, and not what I wanted. But I now know it was really for the highest good. In fact, looking back on any failure, or 'bad event', was actually a good thing. I realize now (especially after reading so much material on the subject), that the Law of Attraction had always been working for me. I had the right attitude, faith, and gratitude to see it through, even though there were moments of doubt and fear. I chose to overcome doubt and fear and stick to my faith.

As you'll see in an upcoming chapter on Belief/Faith, it's probably more important than anything.

As a quick FYI: The 3 books and audio program "The Science of Getting Rich", "Think and Grow Rich", "Creative Visualization", and Tony Robbins' "Personal Power" program were my starting points for this journey. I did not mention all the other success oriented books, CD's, tapes, etc. that I purchased. It really got out of control when a friend lent me his movie "The Secret". My propensity for buying this material was strong, but after viewing "The Secret" I probably tripled my book and CD buying.

But it wasn't necessary. The 3 books and audio program I began with were all I really needed had I followed their instructions initially, and with haste and dedication. I chose to read and listen, take a tidbit or two from each of them, and move forward. If I had followed "Think and Grow Rich" from day one, I know I could have reached my achievements much quicker, and with less *drama*.

During my journey to success, I didn't even know I was using the Law of Attraction. So imagine my *Aha!* moments since it has become so main stream.

This leads me to the true meat of this little book. There are a lot of similar books out there. You probably own some. Have you REALLY followed their instructions? You see I not only believe this stuff works, I'm one of the few success stories that you can learn from, not just read about.

I intend to do this by writing this book, and conveying this material to you as if you and I are sitting on my living room couch having a discussion…Just explaining things to you in plain conversation.

I have never written a book in my life. I don't know any of the authors I've mentioned in this book. I'm getting no kickbacks from anyone. I've put a price tag on this book that's less than what you would pay for one or two gallons of gasoline.

I have no other agenda but for you to use the material in this book to better your life. My purpose is to contribute to the lives of others with my written words.

So I'm taking everything that worked for me. All the information I have read, listened to, seen, and used…And I'm giving it to you in a very short, simple, down-to-earth manner in this book.

My deepest desire is you benefit from this. And then pass it forward...Tell your friends, co-workers, family, everybody...And stop buying all that self-help stuff!

This book will be your last!

Let's begin...

Chapter Two

The Law of Attraction and Creation

Thoughts Become Things

Let's begin with some basics. Your thoughts become things. You can be, do, and have anything you desire. Your thoughts attract like thoughts, ideas, and circumstances. It's all made possible by the Law of Attraction and Creation. I use these two words (attraction and creation) in conjunction with each other because they're pretty much one and the same. (For the sake of reading ease I will use 'LOA' throughout the book from here).

Simply put: You are a magnet.

All creation starts in the mind. If you want to build (create) a new house you first must think of the house in a general sense. Then, by virtue of the LOA you start to attract more like thoughts about the house. The more you focus, the more you continue to attract more thoughts and ideas about the house: structure, size, color, etc.

The thoughts of the house in your mind have a specific frequency, much like a radio has different frequencies. When you tune to a specific radio frequency, you tune in to a specific radio station. So when you tune to a specific frequency in your mind, you get back in return a similar frequency. This frequency is called a vibration, and every creation in the Universe - solid, liquid, gas, etc. has its own distinct vibration. (I will go into deeper detail in a later chapter about vibration).

So any thoughts will attract to it similar thoughts, images, ideas, and so on. You might try thinking of something, anything, right now. Close your eyes and visualize something. As you do, hold that thought's image in your mind for a while. Notice that the longer you hold the image, it begins to expand vividly. Color, size, shape, etc.

These thoughts are energy and attract like energy to it. Everything in the Universe is made of energy. When you break down anything to its purest and simplest form, you get energy.

The interesting thing is, everything in the Universe isn't just energy; it's all made up of the 'same' energy when broken down into its simplest form...Subatomic particles.

Imagine small.
Imagine tiny.
Imagine microscopic.
And keep going.

Seriously...The subatomic particles which make up everything are literally in everything. In other words, the subatomic particles which you are made of are also the same particles in your car, computer, house, air, airplanes, soil, rocks...Well you get the point. These particles are just grouped together differently within every object, gas, liquid, etc.

Okay, so how does this help us get what we want? That life of wealth, health, and happiness. The subject I described above is the basis for Quantum Physics, the energy more commonly known as Quanta, the basic building blocks of the Universe. Also the basis for creating what you want.

A quick, scientific explanation:
Because the Universe is infinite intelligence of which we are all integral aspects, Quanta of energy are influenced by the mind; thought also being pure energy. Whenever you look at a 'possession' such as a house, a car, a computer, they are in fact nothing more or less than an arrangement of energy, or 'Quanta', ultimately created by thought processes of the mind. If these objects were to be inspected very closely, it would be apparent that they are not solid at all, but rather are composed of Quanta of energy vibrating and moving at extremely high rates in and out of the object being observed.

Now, I'm not going deep into the subject...I promised a simple, clear, down-to-earth book. And I meant it. But I felt this must be briefly mentioned because it's important. It's important because our minds; our thought; can control the 'Quanta'.

Do you want me to prove it?
I won't.
Why?

The answers can all be found in any Quantum Physics book you can find at the library or just do an internet search for Quantum Physics, or Quantum mechanics. There's a ton of information on the internet. You'll find the answers you're looking for.

To be perfectly honest, it's unnecessary to understand why or how this stuff works. The power of our minds is far greater than any of us can comprehend, but science is definitely getting closer to understanding.

This book will not teach you all the 'whys' and 'how's'. The purpose of this book is to teach the reader how to create what he/she wants in life. What you want to be, do, or have. Simple. Clear. Down to earth. Let's leave the deep scientific and religious stuff aside.

So let's move on.

Again in simple terms: Thoughts are things.

We use our minds to create what we want. If your desire is to be a dancer, the thought or idea starts out in your mind. You *see* it, or visualize it. As the idea stays in your thoughts you begin to put more focus on it, it expands, and you begin to attract other thoughts pertaining to dancing. Maybe you might ask yourself a question like: "I wonder what it's like to dance in a theater?", or say to yourself: "I love the idea of dancing on Broadway." The idea attracts other thoughts related to it, possibly moving you in the direction of learning how to dance. And perhaps even further, becoming a professional dancer. It starts in the mind.

This applies to every area of our lives. If an idea or thought comes to mind you usually ask yourself internal questions. For example, if you take notice that you're hungry, you might immediately (meaning instantly) ask yourself, "What do I feel like eating?" And maybe a slice of pizza pops into your mind. If there are no internal objections, you might order a pizza or go drive to a pizzeria and buy some.

That's the simple side of it.
You asked for something.
You believed you could/should/will have it.
You took the necessary action to get it.

Too simple? Let's take it a little further...

Let's say you want to be wealthy...A millionaire! But you have a job that only earns $60,000 per year. If you saved every penny you earned, it would take almost 20 years just to get to the first $1,000,000.

However what if you wrote down on a piece of paper the phrase "I'm going to earn $1,000,000 within 2 years." I'm not sure how it's going to happen, but I am definitely going to do it!" You feel it! With purpose and belief!

You affirm (we'll go over affirmations later) this statement to yourself 2-3 times per day.

At the very least, over time, ideas of how you may do this $1,000,000 feat will start to form in your mind. Whether you take action is up to you, but I think you get the point.

In other words, the Law of Attraction is: What you think is what you get.

But in truth that's still way too simple.

Let's pretend you're baking a cake. You need specific ingredients to bake this cake, and there are specific instructions you need to follow.

The LOA is pretty much the same way...

Put in the right ingredients, follow the instructions of the recipe, and manifest your desires.

Now even though different cake recipes do have a few different ingredients, the basic cake recipe holds true...And this also holds true for the LOA. It isn't the Theory of Attraction, or the Nonsense of Attraction. It is the LAW. The Law of Attraction.

In fact, I'm going to use this example of baking a cake as a metaphor for LOA throughout the rest of the book. I'm going to show you:

The equipment you'll need
All the correct ingredients (Desire, Belief, Gratitude, etc.)
Instructions on how to mix them all together.

There will be slight variations to each recipe of course, depending on the individuals desires, but the basic ingredients are always the same.

The real key is to FOLLOW THE INSTRUCTIONS!

In this manner I'm trying to really simplify the manifestation process.

I truly want you to succeed, so the simpler the better.

Let's put our ingredients together...

Chapter Three

Vibration and Being

How You Really Feel

To begin with we need a good mixing bowl into which we can put our ingredients. If you were baking a cake you would want a good, clean bowl. Not a bowl that was dirty, or damaged in some way. What I'm getting at is this...How do you feel? In LOA terms...How are you vibrating? What is your state of being?

I mentioned in the previous chapter about 'vibration'. Everything in the Universe is in motion. Vibrating. Moving. And everything has its own unique frequency. Everything.

Including you!

Let's take a step back...

Quantum Physics shows us that everything in the Universe, when broken down to its simplest form, the subatomic particles, is energy. This energy is unique to everything in existence. That energy is vibrating at a specific and unique frequency. In our minds, if we focus on something long enough it becomes a dominant thought, and we emit the vibration of that thought out to the Universe, which by virtue of the LOA will return to us the like. The LOA states...Like attracts like. Always. Simple.

Or is it simple?

You, and everything else at all given times, are vibrating. What determines your rate of vibration are your emotional states...Your being.

Being is what causes thinking. So if you are happy...Being happy; you will think happy thoughts. You will create happy manifestations. Happiness is your **State of Being**.

Be wealthy. You will think wealthy thoughts. You will create wealthy manifestations. You're vibrating **Being Wealthy**.

How are you vibrating?

How are you **Being**?

If you are Being unhappy it is difficult to manifest something happy or good into your physical reality. How could you? If you wanted to manifest $1,000,000, do you think you should be happy or unhappy? I would bet unhappiness will NOT bring you $1,000,000.

Put another way…If $1,000,000 fell in your lap tomorrow would you be happy or unhappy? Let's assume you'd be happy. You'd also feel wealthy. You'd **Be Wealthy**. You'd **Be Happy**.

The key here is that to attract the money that would make you happy…You must feel that way first! You had to see the money in your mind and how it would make you feel, 'before' it came in to your possession. You may not have realized it. It may have been in your subconscious.

It seems complicated, but it really isn't. It's sort of like this…If I was to ask you what your general, everyday mood is like; you may answer "I feel okay". That is your **Being**. That is your basic 'vibration'. You will basically attract more of that in to your life.

If you asked me the same, I might say "I feel amazing every day!" I am 'being' amazing. I will attract 'amazing' in to my life!

If you feel 'okay' most of the time, and I feel 'amazing' most of the time, which one of us has the better chance of attracting something 'really good' into our lives. This isn't a competition; I'm just trying to prove a point.

Our general state of **Being**(or how we are vibrating) is what the Universe is truly in tune with. If you think life sucks, that's what you transmit to the Universe: it sends back to you things that suck. If you think life is filled with great opportunities, that's what you'll transmit to the Universe: it sends great opportunities to you.

How you are feeling is a measurement of what you're attracting. Feel good. Attract good.

With Being now simplified, I'll ask again…How are you vibrating? How are you Being?

Obviously controlling or guiding the way you think and feel is very important, so I'll devote a small space to it. In a later chapter I will go over how to control your thoughts and feelings through affirmations and questions—your inner speech.

Your Thoughts and Feelings

Positive:
Love, Abundance, Joy, Prosperity, Freedom, Security, Gratitude, Courage, Faith

Negative:
Hatred, Resentment, Envy, Jealousy, Cynicism, Disappointment, Lack, Fear

Both lists above can be much larger, but let's keep it simple.

Ask yourself right now, "In an average day, which thoughts and feelings dominate my mind?" Be honest with yourself.

If the answer is positive thoughts and emotions, you're on the right track. If negative...You MUST change! Plain and simple.

How?

The first step...Decide.

Then take some action. There are numerous actions you can take to go from **being** negative to **being** positive. Some very strong willed people can just decide to do it, and that works for them.

At this point in time in my life I can actually do this. If I'm feeling a bit down and I want to change my state...I say to myself "I choose to feel good right now!" I say this over and over. As I keep saying this, thoughts of feeling good usually enter my mind. I usually see important people in my life smiling and laughing. Just thinking of very positive events does the same thing. A great vacation. Beautiful music.

I don't stop doing this until the momentum of the thoughts takes me to the point of feeling really good. In other words, just putting your thoughts on what you really desire and what feels good in your life can change your state of being.

But there is a simpler way to change your state.

One of the best and easiest 'actions' you can take to change your state is by changing your PHYSIOLOGY. It's not my intention to get into a science lesson, but when you master this simple technique, it will help you change your life. How you are using your physical body can help you change everything. It will take a little practice, but it's painless and very easy.

Let me make this plain and simple...

If you want to change your state from feeling down to feeling good, quickly and easily; change your physical body. Human physiology is the science of the mechanical, physical, and biochemical functions of humans. Our physical bodies very often portray how we're feeling inside.

For example, you might notice that most of the people at a funeral are slumped over, frowns on their faces, looking very depressed, and some even crying. You can tell, just by observing their physical bodies how they feel. Sad. Miserable. The flip side...If you were at a baseball game, and a player for the home team hits a home run, you would then observe many people standing straight up, smiles on their faces, cheering loudly. Again, their physical bodies tell the story.

By changing your physiology, or your physical body, you can instantly change your emotions. Change your vibration. Change your state of being.

Here are some exercises:

1. Standing up straight, with a big smile on your face, ask yourself, "How can I feel good right now?" Say it 20 times in a row, with feeling. Yeah, you look goofy! But so what? Would you rather feel good all day, or bad all day?
2. Stand in front of a mirror and just smile. Don't stop. Think of something really funny. If you can't think of something immediately, be prepared. Watch some funny videos on Youtube.com if you feel down. Watch a comedy on television.
3. Walk around your house with a towel or blanket wrapped around your neck pretending you're Superman. Hey you probably did it when you were a kid, and it was fun wasn't it? So why not now? Even better if your neighbor sees you through a window. Imagine your state after that!!

I think you get the idea. Put a smile on your face. And with a smile on your face I want you to try and feel bad. Sad. Miserable. It's almost impossible! If you put your body in a positive state of being, it's almost impossible to be negative.

And keep doing it until it develops into a habit.

How?

Simply put; the better you feel, the higher your vibration will be...Leading to the happier you'll **Be**. Therefore; the more goodness you'll attract into your life. The more often this happens you will begin to build momentum. The more positive momentum you build up, the easier this all becomes. Eventually you will have a naturally good attitude.

You will **Be** happy!

After that is achieved everything else becomes easy. It will become much easier to manifest what you desire with a positive attitude. A happy state of **Being**.

There are other ways to change your state. The methods I mention work great. In a later chapter I will go over other ways, but I feel they are geared for specific state changes, where the methods listed here are really geared to make you feel good in a general sense.

So we've gone over the equipment we're going to need:

We need you to feel good:

You will have a positive state of 'Being', by 'Vibrating' in a positive, good feeling way;
by thought, or using your 'Physiology' in a positive way.

In other words, you are the mixing bowl. By 'Being' strong, positive, and feeling good, we're ready to start adding our ingredients...

Remember, the better you feel, the better and easier all of this is. Do you think a very wealthy, happy person has a positive outlook on life, or negative? You know the answer. So act as if you are that person.

Choose to feel really good!
Be happy!

Chapter Four

Desire

Burning Desire

Desire is the first ingredient we need to create what we want in life. The desire for more. The desire for better. The desire for different.

What do you really desire?
A better job. A new house. A new car. More friends. Amazing health. More money.

I assume you are reading this book for 1 of 2 reasons:

1. Inspiration
2. You are dissatisfied with one or more areas of your life, and you hope this book contains information to instruct you on how to change that.

First off, I am not writing this solely for inspiration, but I do hope that it inspires people.
Second, if you are dissatisfied in any way, let's go a bit deeper.

You have a desire to change something, or manifest something into your life. Maybe wealth, maybe health, maybe love?
I want you to know something right now…Whatever your desire is; it is absolutely possible that you can have that desire fulfilled. Have no doubts about this!
How strong and powerful is your desire? Is it just a casual want? Or a powerful desire?
Is it…?

"I want a new car"

Or is it...?

"I really love the idea of driving a brand new BMW 550i sedan, in dark blue, with saddle colored leather interior and a V8 turbo engine. I easily see myself cruising along the highway on a beautiful spring day, my favorite music blasting from the speakers, feeling awesome. I love this car!"

There are wants and wishes, and then there is **Burning Desire**. Any thought of truly burning desire erupts in to intense, positive emotion inside of you. You're saying to yourself, "It is a must! I must have this! I must do that. Even though my life is great, if I could get this ____, my life would be many times greater!"

I'm trying to point out to you the role your emotions play in the LOA. If you want to manifest something in your life, you will first need powerful, passionate emotion. A burning desire. You must really feel it!

So if you were to think of getting that new car, shouldn't you just think of it, and it will manifest?

Yes and no.

What's your emotional state? How does the thought of having that car make you feel. You must 'feel' clearly. What I mean is that you need to have specific thoughts and specific emotions. Your emotions surrounding the car should, of course, be positive. Happiness. Excitement. A feeling of success. Joy.

How are you 'vibrating'? Remember the chapter on "Vibrating and Being"? Your emotional state; your vibration, or state of being, is important with desire. It MUST FEEL GOOD! You love the idea of having this brand new, wonderful car, but you hate the idea of paying a high insurance rate, so you're not really in 'high vibration' with manifesting that car. Do you follow? You do have some resistance to the idea.

It must feel good!

Happiness, joy, faith, love, abundance. Do your desires, whatever they may be, bring up these feelings? Or on the other hand, are you allowing your current circumstances to run the show? Are you worried or fearful?

We call that *living by default*. You are not consciously trying to do anything other than 'reacting to' whatever is going on around you. So if you're driving and you see a car accident, chances are you become upset seeing a car crash. You are vibrating being upset, by seeing a car accident. Heavy negative emotions. It plays over and over in your mind. If you focus on these thoughts and emotions long enough, you will attract, and manifest a car accident into your own reality.

That's why I had a chapter on vibration. What is your state of **Being**. Are you happy? Choose to be happy. Are you wealthy? Be wealthy. Do you feel love? Be loving.

Let's take a look at what I call the 'Ugly Side of the Law of Attraction'.

Did you ever get something you didn't want, or have something happen that was bad? For example: were you ever fired from a job? (If not, just go along for the ride). You probably didn't want that to happen, but you did create it in your life.

What??!!

Yeah, I know it's tough to swallow, but if you were ever fired from a job that you wanted to keep, you were the one who really created the circumstances.

It started in your mind and then got coupled with emotion.

To put it in really simple terms: You were afraid of losing your job. Your fear of losing your job brought on the occasional thought(s) of it happening: the 'vibration' of it happening. The emotion gave that vibration power, which brought on more fear, which brought on more thoughts and feelings of it. Then the subconscious, vibrating "Loss Of Job" coupled with fear, caused the manifestation of Job Loss.

I can't believe how many people have said, in a statement to myself and others "I'm afraid I might lose my job or get laid off", only to see it happen weeks or months later. If you think it and you feel it...You get it!

You may not have 'desired' that outcome, but vibration and emotion is what the Universe hears...and always gives. Without exception! What you focus on, especially with strong emotion...You will get.

Now back to desire.

If you really want something and your desire is powerful, and you add positive, passionate emotion, and belief; then that desire, or something even better, sooner or later will come to you. Money, a spouse, a computer, a business, a vacation, a charitable donation, great health, whatever you like.

The first ingredient of the LOA process is to have well thought out, passionate desire. Also, one other thing to touch upon desires...

The clarity or specificity of your desires is very important. The clearer you are about what you want, the easier it is for the Universe to answer your call. If you read the chapter on "My Journey", you'll note I had burning desire, but I lacked clarity. It definitely makes a difference.

"I desire a lot of money"

or

"I am now acquiring $1,000,000, accumulated intermittently over the next 12 months. I envision my life, and the lives of everyone I contact to benefit dramatically from the manifestation of this wealth. I am so grateful!"

If you ask the Universe with confusion, that's what the Universe will give you. If you ask with clarity, you'll get that.

To attain clarity, a simple question or two will do the job...

"Why do I want this money...This job...This spouse? What's the purpose of it?"

Questions like these turn your "I want a lot of money" into "I desire $10,000 to give to a children's hospital, for the highest good of all concerned!"

The more detail you give your desire; the more likely and faster it will manifest.

Well this is just the starting point, and my hope is you come away from this chapter on Desire with the clarity to get started.

I really want you to succeed at this, so I'm putting all of my intention into it.

Ingredient #1

Burning Desire

Next we'll move on to ingredient #2—Belief

This is by far the most important ingredient. I cannot stress that enough!

Let's move on...

Chapter Five

Belief

Faith and Trust

The most important ingredient to create what you want in your life is Belief. Without belief, or faith, or trust; none of this will work 'for you'! I say 'for you' because the LOA is always working...Twenty Four/Seven. It's always working!

Let's take a look at the crazy title of my book, "How I Made $1 Million Using the Law of Attraction". I'm sure many people saw that title and thought, "Well that's just crazy!"

But is it?

First off, are there any people on this planet making $1,000,000 or more, in fewer than 90 days. Of course! If you annualized that income, it's just $4,000,000 per year. Does Warren Buffett, Oprah, Tiger Woods, or any other notable person make that kind of money? Absolutely!

So at the very least, if one person can make that money, the 'possibility' exists. If one person, or 5 people, or 100, or 1000 can do it...Why not you?

Belief!

You have a choice of believing it's possible, or impossible. I just proved it's possible just by naming a few people who do it regularly. Do you believe it's possible for yourself?

I assume the answer is no. If you said yes, I would then assume you just can't wrap your mind around how you could do it, so it's not that different than answering no. I can envision a large number of people saying to themselves "How could I ever make $1,000,000 in

3 months, let alone in 3 years? It's impossible." And I envision their tone being pretty negative.

What if, instead, you asked yourself "How can I make $1,000,000 in 3 months, or 6 months, or 12 months, and really enjoy the process?"

Or,

"How can I manifest $100,000 in 6 months, and really enjoy the process?"

Or,

"How can I earn an extra $5,000 in 3 months, and really enjoy the process?"

How might you reply to yourself? How you speak and reply to yourself, your inner speech is a measurement of your positive or negative attitude and your beliefs.

I re-wrote the questions above 3 times for one reason; I don't know your personal belief about what you think is possible, especially for yourself. But I would bet that each time you read the next question, and the dollar amount kept coming down, it started to become a little more believable. I'd make a second bet that you replied to the third question with at least a "maybe".

If you're going to create the life you really want and deserve, you're going to, at the very least, believe it's possible!

If you don't think it's possible (I didn't say probable) it just won't happen.

Simple? Yes.

Easy? Not so much.

And this applies to any area of life...Health, relationships, prosperity, success, and so on.

But you WANT TO BELIEVE! You want a better life...More money, better health, that amazing relationship. Otherwise you would not be reading this.

What to do?

I am going to show you how to put yourself in a state of believing. You see, your beliefs are just old programming...Stuff you learned unconsciously as a child, as a teenager, young adult, and so on. Things occurred in your life in the past that you chose (probably unconsciously) to believe or not believe.

Two examples of this:

1. A young child, say 6 years old, is running throughout the house. He accidentally knocks over a lamp, and it breaks. The child's mother becomes very upset. In a rage, the mother swats the child's backside, and says "You are a pain in the ass. What a bad kid you are! Go to your room and stay there!" Someone who the child probably respects, trusts, and believes more than anyone else; has just told that child he was bad, and a pain in the rear.
2. A young child, also 6 years old, is running throughout the house. He also accidentally knocks over a lamp, and it breaks. The child's mother comes to the child's side and asks "Are you okay? Don't be upset. We all occasionally make some mistakes. When we make those mistakes (have a failure), we learn and grow from them. It's only a lamp, and can be easily replaced. It will be okay". Someone who the child probably respects, trusts, and believes more than anyone else was just told that occasionally making mistakes can help you learn and grow, and it's okay to make them.

Hmm...What can we assume these two young children, as far as their unconscious beliefs are concerned, have each come away with in their similar circumstances? It's almost as simple as saying child #1 is doomed to failure and unhappiness. Child #2 will try, and try, and try again at life, and at some point succeed with happiness. There's no fear of failure for child #2. Child #1 was scolded for failure.

Even though I made it simple, their beliefs will attract and manifest more of those beliefs as they continue on the paths of their lives; therefore, reinforcing those beliefs in the mind. A kind of domino or snowballing effect, if you will. If you go through life believing (unconsciously) that you're a pain in the butt, or a bad person, more than likely you will have a tough life. And of course the opposite is true. If you think you're a good person, then that will equate to a good life.

Now here is the real beauty of Beliefs...You can change them. Have you heard the statement "The past does not equal the future"?

You DO NOT have to have a certain belief if you choose not to. You choose! Not someone else! Not something that occurred in your past!

Remember I mentioned that you may be similar to myself, and countless others, by continuously buying more and more how-to books, LOA books, how to get rich books, etc. Searching for the 'Holy Grail'.

The 'Holy Grail' is your own belief.

Belief in what is possible for you.

Belief that this process can and will work for you.

Belief in the Law of Attraction and Creation.

Belief you create your reality.

Belief that the Universe loves and supports you.

Belief in yourself.

The beauty of belief...Anything is possible!

So how do you change your beliefs to unwavering trust and faith?

How about a little at a time...Starting out real small in the beginning and then using the evidence of what occurs to continue to build on itself, until you so thoroughly believe that anything is possible you will be unstoppable! Your dominant thought will be belief! Positive momentum!

So if you're ready, I will tell you a short personal Belief story of my own, and how I used the evidence of what occurred to build huge momentum. I will describe exactly what I did, and how you can do the same.

*****

The Blue Feather

When I first saw the movie "The Secret", I was intrigued, but doubtful about the subject matter. I picked up a handful of books about the Law of Attraction by a few different authors, and became even more intrigued. Up until then I had read a large amount of self-help and how-to books, and felt I had success with the ideas presented in them. However, this Law of Attraction theory was a real step beyond my belief.

I create my entire reality?

I can manifest anything in my life with just thought? I saw it, not so much as religious or spiritual, but more based in science (Quantum Physics); with spirituality sort of on the fringe...

I think I had a hard time swallowing the deeper meanings of what I had been learning. I guess even though a great deal of the material that I had read about creating success by being positive, happy, and deliberate, had kind of mentioned the Law of Attraction; but the sheer Power of LOA brought a lot of doubts and fears into my mind.

If I just think of illness I may, or will, become sick. This scared me! (At first)

Maybe I didn't want to believe my mind was that powerful. But if my mind really is that powerful, I also realized the incredible potential that existed.

I needed to prove this 'LOA stuff' to myself. I needed to believe that this stuff really worked. Because if it did, I knew I had to start having a deeper control of directing my thoughts. The basis was: If negative thoughts almost always produce negative results, and the opposite is also true; then truly directing my thoughts could bring about amazing things! But being reactive to negative events or surroundings could result in negative thoughts and feelings, resulting in disaster!

Awesome! And Yikes!

I was excited and fearful, but realized if this is Universal Law which works no matter what, and all the time; I chose to accept it, and use it to my advantage. But I needed some evidence; some proof.

So I decided to try and manifest something by using only my mind, and allowing those 'happy coincidences' to occur. I would not spend money or take any physical action to acquire my desired manifestation, because that would defeat the purpose of the experiment. I wanted to manifest something that I 'believed' could/would happen. But it had to be something so unusual that I would be convinced it was NOT a coincidence.

Believe it or not, I went searching on the internet for an idea with the question running through my mind "What can I attract into my life that will instill belief in the Law of Attraction?" I ended up coming upon a story of some man who was also seeking the same result I was (Coincidence?). He attempted to manifest a blue feather into his life. This actually worked for him. I decided to try the same thing.

I couldn't recall seeing a blue feather in years, let alone a bird feather of any color. Yes I see birds all the time, but never an individual feather; and certainly not a blue one. I also realized I had no use for a blue feather, so I wasn't interested in buying one or somehow taking physical action to do so.

The experiment was on!

I first wrote down my desire...This is a powerful way to kick your subconscious into gear. I wrote:

"I am so happy and grateful that a beautiful, blue feather is now manifesting into my life. It manifests in simple and easy ways, for the highest good of all concerned."

Over the next few days I would awaken a bit early in the morning, close my eyes, and visualize a blue feather. I saw its shape; it's color. I felt its texture. I envisioned laughing to the tickling feeling when I touched it to my neck. In my mind I already had the blue feather; by using my imagination. I did this visualizing again in the afternoon, and again at bedtime. I occasionally thought about it, very casually, throughout my day...always giving the thought positive feeling energy.

I did this for 3 days. And some things began to happen...

First, on Day #3 of the experiment, I was watching television in the evening when a television commercial came on. At the end of the commercial, a feather was shown floating in the air. I thought "Hey, that's interesting", and then pretty much dismissed it as a coincidence.

Second, on Day #4, I had been outside when it started to downpour. I ran into the house and noticed my son and daughter were watching "Forrest Gump" on television. I happened to walk in at the very end of the movie, when it shows a feather blowing around in the breeze. This time I did not dismiss this as coincidence. I thought "That's very interesting!" It felt almost as if someone was trying to tell me something (like a hunch, or strong intuition).

Third, later that same day...We invited friends over for dinner that evening. It had rained all day, and the ground was soaked. When our friends arrived, my male friend came inside the house and brushed his feet back and forth on my "Welcome" mat. I remember this because he did it comically, the way a cartoon character might do it. When he stepped off the mat, there it was. It must have been on the bottom of his shoe, and he brushed it onto the mat. A big feather...But it was gray, not blue!

I wasn't sure what to think. I wanted to manifest a blue feather. I visualized as instructed from my readings. I saw signs or coincidences, that the Universe was sending me what I asked for, but this wasn't what I asked for. It almost was. Hmm...I pondered.

Over the next 2 days I really didn't use my visualization techniques. I did them, but it was more by rote. Very mechanical; passionless. I did think about the blue feather. It popped in my mind from time to time. I hadn't seen anything since the gray feather. I just sort of forgot everything about it for the moment, caught up in my day to day agenda.

On Day #6, I had gotten up at 6:30am, did NOT do visualization for the feather. I worked for about 4 hours, and then decided to get a haircut. I walked out of the house to drive to my barber. I got in my car and started her up. I was about to back out of the driveway, when suddenly; two huge blue jays, fighting like wildcats, landed on my windshield, grappling and pecking at one another. They scared the heck out of me! I quickly thought to scare them by beeping my horn. Upon hearing the noise, they got scared and flew away.

On the windshield it sat; bright and colorful, like a cloudless sky. A big, blue jay feather. You may have heard of AHA! moments, epiphanies, and quantum leaps. This was mine! Any bit of doubt that I had about this Law of Attraction stuff...Was gone!

I still have that feather in a small frame above my desk; as a reminder that anything is possible. Faith, Hope, Trust...Belief!

*****

The point of the "Blue Feather" story is it gave me strong enough evidence to believe.

Belief is key.

I did some more experiments very similar to this. They all had similar results. The purpose was simple; I wanted to keep seeing evidence that this really worked. Repetition is the mother of skill. Repetition convinced my subconscious. Every time I saw evidence that LOA worked, my mind's beliefs became stronger and stronger.

I also decided to keep what I call "My Evidence Journal". I would absolutely advise you to do the same. I write down any bits of *'evidence'* of manifestations. The more you see, the more you write, the deeper you believe. You will eventually have a very deep belief about what is really possible. No, not just possible, but probable. It becomes ingrained on your subconscious.

So start to experiment.

Start small:
Try to use your imagination to visualize something into your life. Write it down, close your eyes, and use your imagination.
It must be believable to you...So again, start small. Make it something easy.
Use an evidence journal and write down your results.

In an upcoming chapter I will put emphasis on your imagination, and using visualization techniques. They're pretty simple, but visualization must be mastered to create what you desire in your life...Using your imagination.

In the meantime, just think of something simple you desire and believe it's already yours.

You'll be amazed!

Ingredient #2

Belief

Next we'll move on to our 3rd and 4th ingredients, which sort of coincide with one another: Allowing/Receiving with Gratitude.

Let's go...

Chapter Six

Allowing and Receiving

Gratitude is the Key

First we have Desire---Asking
Then we have Belief---Believing
Now we have Allowing---Receiving

We asked the Universe for something with a burning Desire, and you Believe that you already have your desire using your imagination (visualizing). Now you must receive it. You must allow it into your physical experience.

Sounds simple enough. But this is where people; a lot of people, blow it.

Why?

A number of reasons. Maybe they were impatient. Maybe they didn't have enough belief. Maybe their desire is not that strong. Or maybe they became so focused on NOT seeing the desire in physical form that they were actually focused on the lack of it. Aha!

That is the biggest reason you're not getting what you want. Impatience is mixed in a bit, which causes you to focus on the lack of something. Your desire isn't manifesting fast enough for your taste.

If you envision having that shiny new car sitting in your driveway and your desire is strong, and you keep imagining, but every time you look out at the driveway you *'notice'* it not being there…even for a moment; your notice of the 'lack of a new car' is the vibration your broadcasting out to the Universe; and it gives you what you are asking for…Lack of a new car. You are attracting lack.

This is very common, especially when first trying to deliberately create.

Stumped? Stymied? How about pissed off!?

And what to do?

Remember about **Vibration and Being**...Feeling good!

Add one more ingredient:

Gratitude!

To add Gratitude into our mixing bowl with Desire and Belief is of utmost importance. Gratitude is the Champion of Emotions. Gratitude is kind of like the compilation of every positive feeling you can have. In fact, without gratitude your state of **being** is unhappy on some levels.

If you feel confident; you feel grateful!

If you feel abundant; you feel grateful!

If you feel happy; you feel grateful!

Are you practicing gratitude in your life? Are you a grateful person? Think about how you're vibrating. How are you feeling?

Well, if you're having an unusually tough time in your life you may be struggling to feel grateful. Maybe you lost your job, or have very little money. So you say to yourself "I have nothing to be grateful for! Life sucks!"

However, you can overcome these negative emotions by finding something small to be grateful for, and instantly change your state from sadness, depression, and worry to happiness, hope, and love. I always recommend starting with PHYSIOLOGY first, because it's easy to do. If you are still struggling to feel grateful, there's more you can do.

Let's start by looking at how you start your day...

When you awaken in the morning, what's the first thought or feeling you awaken to?

Maybe it's "Why do I have to get up and go to my crappy job?", or "What am I happy (grateful) about in my life this morning?" I think it is obvious which question will bring up good thoughts and feelings, and which won't. (As you can tell by now, I'm big on asking one's self the right questions. So Important!)

Wouldn't you agree with me; regardless of your current situation, waking up and starting your day feeling grateful, instead of miserable will probably attract and manifest good things into your life? Wouldn't you also agree with me that you actually have a choice?

You do!

You are the only one who gets to choose whether you are happy or sad!

A quote from Groucho Marx (1890-1977), the famous Comedian and Film Star:

"Each morning when I open my eyes I say to myself: I, not events, have the power to make me happy or unhappy today. I can choose which it shall be. Yesterday is dead, tomorrow hasn't arrived yet. I have just one day, today, and I'm going to be happy in it."

So the saying goes: Live with an attitude of gratitude.

Be grateful for something in your life. Be grateful for the oxygen you breathe. Be grateful for all the food that fills supermarket shelves. Be grateful for the mind you have. Be grateful for the laughter of children.

There must be something you can be grateful for. And why the big deal about Gratitude?

When you focus on gratitude...When you are **'Being Grateful'**, by virtue of the Law of Attraction, you will attract more things into your life to be grateful for!

So once again...Ask the right question:

Why am I so grateful?

What is there to be grateful for in my life?

Why am I so lucky? (This particular question works well for me...Makes me realize how truly lucky I am to have my life).

Mix Gratitude in with Desire and Belief...This equals Positive, Passionate, Power! Which equals...I can be, do, and have anything!

I guess I'm trying to stress, once again, one very important thing:

You must feel good in order to create what you desire. If you feel grateful, and see things that occur in your life as blessings instead of burdens, your life changes for the better. Massively!

Be grateful for what is, and be grateful for what's coming. Remember you created it.

And if you created what is, then you are creating what will be. If you are grateful for what is, you will create things to be grateful for.

I'll repeat that:

You created your now. 'Your' moment right now. You created this moment in time. Somewhere, sometime in the past, you created your now. So be grateful for it! The more grateful you are for what is: you will create a future to be grateful for. Do you get that?

If you're grateful for what was, and grateful for what is, and grateful for what's coming...

That's positive expectation!!

That is not feeling frustrated because that shiny new car hasn't shown up. That's being excited for the time when the car does show up. Do you see the difference?

That is the difference between a person who deliberately creates their future and someone who keeps getting stuck.

Expect the best. Be happy about it. Be grateful. And you will ALLOW into your life your deepest desires. That is how you RECEIVE your desires. You ALLOW them in by having positive expectations through gratitude.

And it's easy to tell if you're allowing, or not.

By how you feel: Your emotions!

If you feel great, you are allowing. If you feel rotten, you are resisting. It's that simple. So pay attention to how you feel, and adjust your thinking and emotions accordingly! I continue to stress how important your emotional **being** is.

Finally, to quote a sentence from "The Science of Getting Rich":

"The reason to be grateful":

"The mental attitude of gratitude draws the mind in to closer touch with the source from which the blessings come".

So where are we so far?
Let's sum up what we've got...

Desire
Belief
Gratitude
Vibration or Being

In simple terms...In order to manifest your desires, you have to be in a state of gratitude, or happiness. You must have a strong desire, and believe that you can, will, and deserve what you desire.

By being in a state of gratitude, or being grateful, you should, by virtue of the Law of Attraction, attract and manifest all things in your life to be grateful for!

In other words...

Be Joyful!
Be Grateful for that Joy!
You will attract more of it!

It really is that simple!

Let's move on to the tried and true methods that I personally use to make that all possible...

Chapter Seven

Inner Speech

How You Speak to Yourself

This chapter alone...all by itself, can change your life.

Have you ever called yourself a bad name? Let's say you spilled a drink on the floor, and you immediately said to yourself "I'm such an idiot!" Or something even worse.

We've all done this.

But are you really an idiot? Or worse?

My assumption is that you're not. But in an instant, during some accident or mistake, you chose to become one. You chose to beat up on yourself. You chose to condemn yourself; put yourself down.

This is your inner speech. How you speak to yourself determines how you feel But more importantly; how you feel about yourself.

How about: "Why doesn't anything work out for me?"

If a person spends most of their time with that question on their mind, what do you think they will attract and manifest in their lives?

How about: "Why am I so comfortable with money?"

Ask yourself that question 10 times an hour, for 15 hours per day, for 4 weeks. I think you'd be surprised by the outcome.

The point is; how we speak to and with ourselves is one of the most important things in our lives. If we do it the right way, on a conscious level, for a long enough time; it becomes a habit, and we simultaneously reprogram our subconscious mind.

A habit is a behavior run by the subconscious. We don't really think about it once it becomes a habit. Like driving a car. When I was 17 I had to think about every little thing when driving. Thirty years later, I don't think about driving at all...My subconscious runs the whole show. If you've been driving for more than a year or two you know what I mean.

Which habit do you desire?

"How come I never have enough money", or

"Why am I so comfortable with money?"

I know it's a rhetorical question. But it's got you thinking, doesn't it?

Do you ever say "It figures!?"

This normally means you are responding to something you perceive as bad or negative. Your reaction "It figures!" says a lot about your thinking. About your **being**. In other words, it's no surprise to you that something bad happened. In fact you expected it. You have negative expectations. You're **being** negative!

Now, first the bad news (if you choose to see it that way)...

You created, or co-created it.

Yes, You.

If you are the person who says "It figures!" you have a negative outlook, or what I call a negative 'flow' on things. The Law of Attraction does not care. If your attitude is one of negative expectations; you will get what you ask for. It Is The Law!

Here's the good news...

This is old programming...You learned things over numerous years of experiences, unconsciously. You heard it, saw it, felt it. The subconscious soaked it up like a sponge, and now it's just an unseen habit of thinking. You are transmitting those thoughts and feelings to the Universe, which it returns back to you in physical equivalent. You probably, until now, never realized you were doing this.

With this self-realization, you can reprogram yourself. It's actually pretty easy. You are going to change your inner speech, and treat yourself, through your words and thoughts, with love, respect, and kindness.

When you accomplish this, even in a small way; your life will become so joyful and fulfilling that you will become unstoppable. A creator of your own destiny. You will **'BE'** what you want to **'BE'**! Why? Because if you love, respect, and honor yourself; the Universe will return those things to you. And if you know that love, respect, and honor are always on the way to you...Just imagine what you might manifest into your life!

This is 'WHY' we are here: For Joy. For Happiness! Not suffering and misery.

So let's get started on changing you (if you need changing)...Through you inner speech. Now I don't know you personally, so you're going to have to have a little self-acknowledgment; be honest with yourself, and see where you stand with this.

You are going to have to become conscious of your inner-talk; your thoughts. Take the time to be conscious of your thinking. When I first began noticing my self-talk I used a trick or two to see if I 'liked' what I was saying to myself. In other words; was it negative and pessimistic, or positive and optimistic? I would pretend that instead of talking/thinking to myself, I was actually talking to my Grandmother. Kind of funny, but hear me out.

Quick Story:
A contractor was working at my home. He was cutting wood with a power saw, when he accidentally sliced the extension cord in half. He became so angry. He started yelling "God, I'm such an a__hole"!

I heard him and ran over, thinking he was hurt. He kept on screaming over and over again "God, I'm such an a__hole!" When he quieted down a bit I asked him "Why are you saying such things? Would you talk that way to your grandmother?!"

He stopped everything. I don't think he expected to hear anything like that. Then I said, "Wow, you're really lucky. That could have been your hand instead of just a $10.00 extension cord that you sliced. Don't beat yourself up for a small accident or mistake. In fact, that will probably never happen again because you learned something. Have more respect for yourself, you're a good guy" I finished.

And that's the point...Speak to yourself with respect, kindness, and love. The way you would speak to your Grandma. Or pretend your speaking to a 9 month old baby. I've tried that with great success also.

Get the point?

In other words…Stop and Think! Learn to catch yourself from this self-deprecating behavior, and then turn it into positive and uplifting speech.

"Why am I so lucky?"

"How did I get so lucky?"

"How is it I take such good care of myself?"

"Why am I so healthy?"

"Why does the Universe love me so much?"

Get it? Good.

So the next time a situation arises, take a deep breath, and affirm a positive statement. Or ask a better question. Make it a habit and those *'situations'* won't come up very often.

In the meantime, using affirmations and empowering questions, in a repetitious manner throughout your day, from morning until night; will work wonders for your attitude and outlook on life.

This is very important! You direct your thoughts with your inner speech. So direct that speech.

All day.

Yes, all day…Until it becomes a habit.

Simple?

Yes!

Easy?

That depends...

The reality here is this…You must develop self-control. Controlling your inner speech leads to controlling your thoughts. This leads to controlling your life! If you choose that it's easy to do; then it is. If you choose that it will be difficult; then it will be. There's no wrong answer.

So throughout your day say positive affirmations to yourself…Ask yourself empowering questions. Force yourself. Control yourself.

If you truly want to have that great life you dream about, you must take responsibility for your own well-being. So take responsibility by always speaking to yourself positively.

I did, and still do.

It works!

Follow my instructions. I know it seems simplistic. You know what? It is. You shouldn't think any of this stuff is complicated, because it isn't. That's the beauty of my little book. It's simple. The other books on the same subject are usually very wordy, but have the same material. Please don't fool yourself into believing you need a 400 page tome on the subject of LOA to make it work for you. Please trust me.

This stuff is simple.

Positive Affirmations

Here is a list of positive affirmations you can use. If nothing here resonates with you, I would advise you to do an internet search. Type in positive affirmations on www.Google.com (or whatever you prefer), and you should find something you can use.

But allow me to offer you one piece of advice...The best affirmations are the ones you come up with on your own. I believe that your subconscious will respond best to your own creativity. So just use the list below as a guideline, if possible.

- I am confident that everything always goes my way.
- Every day, in every way, I am getting better and better.
- I am the master of my life.
- I love money, and money loves me.
- I love and appreciate myself just as I am.
- It's okay for me to have everything I want.
- I enjoy relaxing and having fun.
- The more I have, the more I can give.
- I know the Universe loves and supports me.
- I am open to receiving all the blessings of the Universe.
- I choose to be happy, right now!
- I am now enjoying everything I do.
- I have a great and loving relationship with ____.
- I am successful in whatever I do.
- I am well.(Confident, happy, loving, etc.)
- My body heals quickly and easily. I have perfect health.
- I always have more than enough money. (This is a favorite of mine)
- My mind is finely tuned for attracting massive wealth.

- Money (Abundance, Prosperity, Success) flows to me easily and generously.
- I am a magnet to money.
- I have unbreakable confidence in myself.
- I am thankful for the abundance in my life.
- I can be whatever I will to be.

You get the point! Find what feels best for you.
A great starting point on the internet:
www.freeaffirmations.org

Empowering Questions

This is an area you don't hear too many self-help practitioners talk about. But if you want better answers, ask better questions. Empowering questions is a step above affirmations. The reason I say that is because of the way your mind functions. Your mind, when it receives information like an affirmation, may immediately deny that affirmation.

For example, if you repeat to yourself several times "Money comes to me easily and generously", your mind may immediately respond "Oh yeah! Look at your bank statement!"

However, when an empowering question is used, the mind will justify its response. "Why does money always flow to me so easily and generously?" Now the mind replies much more positively, because you are presupposing the positive part of the question is already true.

I personally ask myself questions constantly. It was the first method I learned about how to change my state.

I start with general how-to type of questions...

"What am I grateful for in my life?"

"How can I earn more money, and enjoy the process?"

"How can I earn more money, and help others in the process?"

I also use empowering questions depending on what area of my life I'm trying to improve...

"How is it that I'm so confident?"

"Why does everything always go my way?"

"Why am I so comfortable with money?"

I usually end up answering these questions in my mind with powerful affirmations. It works great!

The following is a short list of empowering questions. The simplest method for coming up with an empowering question is to take a positive affirmation that fits your needs, and just rearrange it into a question. Also, use the internet search query 'empowering questions'.

- What am I grateful for in my life?
- What can I do to make myself happy? (and enjoy the process?)
- What steps can I take that will move me toward my ideal career?
- Why am I so healthy?
- Why do I take such good care of myself?
- Why am I so comfortable with money?
- How is it that things always go my way?
- How do I solve this problem I have, and enjoy the process? (More money, better health)
- Why am I so amazing? (Magnificent, fantastic, awesome, etc.)
- Why does God (The Universe, Source, Creation) love me so much?
- What is great about this?
- What can I learn from this?
- How is it that I always have all the right answers?
- How is it that I'm so loved?

I think you get the idea.

Asking yourself empowering questions, especially presupposed questions, is an extremely powerful tool to use to help create your desires.

So try the affirmations and questions. Get a feel for them. And practice, practice, practice. Repetition is key here. That means "SAY THEM ALOT"! You are using them to reprogram your unconscious mind, so it may take a lot of repetition to have it sink in.

When to use them?

With questions and affirmations...I tend to do them after I awaken, and right before bedtime. This is the time your subconscious is more open to suggestion. I especially like to use "I am" affirmations as I lay in bed falling asleep.

"I am happy."
"I am wealthy."
"I am well."

I repeat them over and over until I fall asleep. It's great to program your subconscious when it's most receptive, so this works great for me. It should for you, too.

Throughout the day, I tend to use 'generalized' questions and affirmations, just to keep my mind working. And deliberately creating what I want.

So in other words, I always use them. Continuously feeding the mind with positive phrases, and asking the mind positive questions, will lead to new positive beliefs. And once you use them regularly, it becomes such a habit you don't even realize you're doing it anymore!

Have fun with it!

Chapter Eight

The Imagination

Using Visualization Techniques to Create

Finally! The real meat and potatoes of my little book: Techniques to create what you desire.

We have the most important equipment and ingredients:

Equipment:
    Vibration
    Being
    Physiology
Ingredients:
    Desire
    Belief
    Gratitude (Allowing)

Now there is more equipment we could add, and there are other ingredients, but they're always different and depend on the individual, as well as the individual desire. For now, let me show you the basic techniques of using your imagination, and the best, simplest method of visualizing what you want. If used regularly, the first visualization technique is all you really need. I have gotten incredible results from just using the basic technique alone.

It's very simple.

First- Desire

Ask yourself what you would like. In the beginning, keep it small and believable. We'll build up to bigger things as your belief grows. Write this Desire down on paper; maybe in a journal. For example "I am so happy and grateful now that an extra $500.00 has manifested in my life."

Second– Get comfortable and relax

Sit in a comfortable chair, or lie down. Make sure you won't be disturbed. Relax. Breathe deeply 2-3 times. What I do is close my eyes, and say to myself "The top of my head is now relaxed." Then "My ears are relaxed." "My eyes are relaxed." I take a deep breath. "My nose is relaxed". I work my way down to shoulders, chest, thighs, and so on down to my toes. "My whole body, from head to toe, is relaxed, and feels really good." Breathe deeply.

Then I say to myself "I am going to count down from 10 to 1. When I reach the number 1, I am going to be in a very deep, relaxed state, and feel really good." Then slowly count backwards from 10 to 1, continuing to breathe deeply. You should feel pretty relaxed now.

Third– Belief

Now start to imagine what your Desire is. The more specific; the more clarity you give the image in your mind, the more powerful it will be. Imagine yourself with your Desire. Really see yourself with the object, or person, or situation you desire. Use your imagination. You must **FEEL** as if you already have it! For example, if you desire an object, see yourself touching or holding it, see its color and size. Does it have a smell? A Taste? A Sound? Imagine how having this object makes you feel. Have fun with this! Live it in your mind as if it's real. Because it is to your subconscious. Now.

Fourth– Positive Statement

You can say, in your mind or out loud, some strong, good feeling statements about your Desire. "I really love having this, being here, owning this." (There is an entire chapter on affirmations and self-talk.)

Fifth– Time

The time you feel comfortable doing this is up to you. As a guideline I would recommend starting out with a few minutes, and slowly build it up to 10-15 minutes. I tend to do this for about 15 minutes, 2-3 times per day. I especially like doing it just before bedtime...It's very easy to relax when you're going to sleep.

Sixth– Ending Statement

I always end my visualization session with a statement. "This (your desire), or something even better, now manifests for me, in easy and harmonious ways, for the highest good of all concerned."

I use this statement so it puts the Universe on 'alert' that I'm open to something even better happening if possible, and that it benefits everyone involved.

That is the basic visualization technique.
Quite simple.

Some pointers:
- Your subconscious mind does not know whether you are imagining, or if it's real. So when you imagine, the Universe (God, Creation, Source) receives those thoughts and images as though you were actually living them. The Universe must return those visions to you.
- The stronger your conscious Belief during the visualization; the easier it is for your subconscious to believe as well, and the sooner your Desire will manifest...Or at least you may see 'coincidences'.
- These 'coincidences'...You must be open to them. Think of my "Blue Feather" story. The Universe was 'hinting' or 'talking to me' that my Desire was on its way.
- Feel GOOD! Positive emotions, as strong as possible, will make the process fun, fulfilling, and easier.
- Ask questions– "How can I feel good while doing my visualizations? Why does this process feel so awesome?"
- Practice, Practice, Practice!
- Believe
- Believe
- Believe...I can't stress this enough! Even if you believe 99%, that 1% of doubt may act as a barrier to your Desire manifesting. Just decide to give it your all!!

Okay...That is the basic visualization technique. Another similar technique is below:

1. Desire (write it out)

2. Relax

3. Instead of imagining a vision (you will accidentally), use spoken words, aloud or in your mind. When you do this you will see mental pictures anyway, so it is similar. The key here is to speak with powerful intention. Passionate. Unwavering.
Example:
"I am so happy and grateful for my new _____ job. It's so fulfilling, rewarding, and creative. I now see my life getting better and better, everyday!"

4. Repeat, like a mantra or affirmation. The repetition is what brings up emotions and images into your mind.

5. You may even combine the 2 techniques; whatever makes you feel comfortable and feels good to you!

Using either one of these techniques will work wonders in your life. They have for mine. This is also the area where people fail. Most folks don't want to do this. They consider it work, or too time consuming. But let me ask you this...
What are you doing now to create what you want in your life?
And how's that working for you? If it's not, put some faith in this method.

It works!

Chapter Nine

More Information

Tips, Pointers, and Other Help

If you've read any other personal development books, self-help books, or Law of Attraction books; you've probably noticed I've left some things out that are contained in similar material that you probably expected to see here. But as I noted in the beginning of this book, I really wanted to give the reader a very simple, clear, no-nonsense book.

My intention was this; I asked myself the following questions:

"What works now, and has worked for me in the past? How can I relay this to a person or group of people as simply as possible? Can someone use this information immediately without feeling overwhelmed or confused? What information am I aware of that a person really *doesn't* need to make positive changes in their life?"

I really wanted you to feel like we were sitting on a couch in my living room, and we were having a conversation. Simple. Easy to understand.

The preceding material meets all that criteria. But I also want you to know there are plenty of other resources available related to the subjects of personal development and the Law of Attraction. In this final chapter I will touch briefly on a number of inter-related subjects. You deserve to be aware of them, because many can be great tools to help you.

I advise you to search them up on the internet at your convenience.

The Universe
Source Energy
Creation
Infinite Intelligence
God

    This particular area is one I decided to avoid at all costs. My hope is that every reader looks inside of themselves before looking outside of themselves. What I'm trying to say is; every person has a particular belief about how the Universe, or the Source, or Infinite Intelligence, or God works; mostly in spiritual terms. Because there are such varying beliefs, I thought it best to have the reader decide for his or her self.
    I have no desire to alienate anyone's religious or spiritual beliefs.
    I believe that the Universe (my "word" for the loving creator of all that is) loves us, supports us, and wants the best for us. There are Natural Laws of the Universe; the most powerful of course is the Law of Attraction. I believe that we have complete freewill. We decide what kind of life we are going to have, and the Universe completely supports that by use of the Law of Attraction.
    Many books and practitioners TELL you what you SHOULD believe on this subject. So do many different religions. My question is "Who is right? Who gets to decide?"
    Well, you do.
    So whatever makes you feel best...I say go with it.
    In my opinion, I believe we are here for one reason only...Joy.
    Whatever you have to do to have a joyous life...DO IT!

The Flow of the Universe

What do I mean by *The Flow*? Have you, or someone you know ever been in a boat on a river? It's pretty common knowledge that a river 'flows' in one direction. If a person tries to paddle his boat against that 'flow', termed "paddling upstream", they tend to struggle. It can be quite difficult.

The Universe 'flows' quite similarly. It grows. It expands. It moves in the direction of goodness. I'm sure there are moments in your life where things were fun and easy, and other times difficult and painful. I am of the belief that if you have difficulty and pain, you are paddling upstream, against the current. I believe that life should be easy and fun. Joyful. Pleasant.

The term "go with the flow" is what I'm getting at. If you're struggling in any way, you are moving against the *'current'* or *'flow'* that is best for you. You're fighting the Universe. You're fighting yourself. If you are unhappy about something (against the *'flow'*), ask yourself "What can I do to feel good?" Put yourself in a position to go with the flow.

To decide, or desire to move against this *'flow'*, is called Resistance.

Resistance

You are resisting what is best for you. Your emotions; how you're feeling, are key indicators of "resisting or allowing". If you are resisting, you feel bad, or angry, or disappointed, etc. You feel some kind of negative emotion.

This resistance, or negative feeling, should be your major concern. When you resist you obviously can't manifest what you want. How many people in the world 'RESIST' being wealthy? Resist abundance. Resist prosperity.

A lot!

Why?

If you think about money or success and you feel a negative emotion about it, you are resisting money, or success, or great health, or whatever. You associate 'something' painful to it. You're blocking it.

Let's just discuss money since it's such a hot topic. This applies to anything: health, relationships, and so on. We'll use money as a key example. The reason you don't have enough money, or you don't earn enough money, or you have a ton of debt is simple...You resist it. You resist it unconsciously. This is usually caused by something(s) that occurred in your past that your subconscious believed to be true.

An example of this might be that your parents instilled in you the thought that "Money is the root of all evil", or "Money doesn't grow on trees". If you were to hear those phrases continuously, and with enough emotion, your unconscious mind will believe it. It would then be no surprise that as your life progressed; you would struggle financially until you were able to clear that resistance.

In today's society, the media makes the wealthy and rich seem like Satan's disciples. Do you realize how much good the wealthy actually do for our world? Just the fact that they own the businesses that supply jobs to countless millions would be the least. But yet the media finds one bad apple in the bunch and turns it into a circus, making the wealthy seem like terrible people.

If your subconscious, for any reason, thinks its "BAD" to have money; you will struggle until you can clear that belief. If you think having money will make you a terrible person, you will resist money. You are 'vibrating' that money is terrible. Keep it away from me. I don't want to be terrible.

This goes for any desire: Great health, a happy loving relationship, a business, and so on.

Ask and it is given. The Universe is just responding to your request!

The beliefs around money (or any desire)...The resistance you have, must be changed.

How?

Change the belief. Clear the resistance. (The chapter on Belief touches upon this)

Clearing

Even though we've touched upon clearing out old beliefs by using and changing your inner speech, as well as using your physiology; there are other clearing methods you may find useful. If you're really struggling to make some changes, and you can't seem to direct your thoughts and emotions; I would guess you have really powerful resistance. If you feel this is so, the resistance MUST be cleared out in order for you to move forward.

Let me say this...You may need some help to clear your resistance: Anything from success coaching or life coaching, and possibly even therapy. You know yourself better than anyone.

I personally believe we all have the ability within ourselves to solve any problem that we face; to create what we want in our lives. Unfortunately, some people just can't gain control of their lives without some form of help.

Don't be afraid to seek out help if you think you need it. Whatever can help you, the Universe will provide it!

Going back to Clearing...

I'll list some clearing exercises for those of you who desire to go beyond the physiology and inner speech exercises I gave you in those preceding chapters.

Whenever I have used a clearing exercise I usually begin with a question. For example:

"The reason I can't have _____ is because"...and then I list what comes up.

"The reason I can't have a new car is because":
- I don't deserve it
- I have no money
- It's too difficult to get

And so on...Whatever comes up, thoughts or emotions, now will be dealt with. Do not repress them, or try to change them. That has NOT been working for you, so let's try to clear them instead.

Write the question, and list down on paper. (This wakes your mind)

First and simplest, is emotional clearing.

Emotional Clearing:

Emotional Clearing is the practice of bringing awareness to our mental and emotional compulsions and reactions in order to "heal" them or integrate them.

1. Stop resisting the negative sensations in your body. Instead, bring awareness to your body and allow it to inform you.
2. Stop resisting your emotions. Instead, bring awareness to them and allow them. (We avoid actually feeling our emotions by projecting them and repressing them. This must stop to actually clear them.)
3. Stop resisting and repressing negative thoughts. Instead, observe them and question them.
4. Once you achieve the 3 steps above, continue to do this and actually allow all this to be okay. Let it inform you about its origins.
5. Follow the sensations, feelings, and thoughts - beliefs to their origins in your childhood. Allow all the related negative conditions and experiences to be okay. This will create a state in which the original formative traumatic or overwhelming incident will naturally begin to "heal" or resolve.
6. Allow all of this to soften and flow in, around and out of your body space, while holding your early childhood self in a nurturing embrace.
7. Continue to do this until you feel a great release of energy and possibly an essential state like "inner peace".

This clearing exercise is very common, and simple. It may take a bit of practice, but don't give up. You may have some catharsis before it's over, but you will feel great afterward.

Other clearing methods:

The Silva Method…www.silvamethod.com
The Sedona Method…www.sedonamethod.com

I'm listing these 2 methods as web searches. I have looked in to them, but never used either one. I've heard they are very similar. I never felt the need, so I never tried them. Many people swear by one or the other. I would say to you, if one interests you, check it out. Do some homework. Since I never tried either, I won't recommend either. But that doesn't mean they don't work. I would hate that one could help you, and I didn't at least mention it. You may find what you need to clear blocks from one of these two methods, and then move forward to huge growth. There's more info onwww.youtube.com.

One last clearing method called Emotional Freedom Technique, or the Tapping Method, I have actually used and had great results with. I was actually quite surprised, since the method is quite 'goofy' looking when done. I was extremely skeptical about this method when I first heard about it, but I'm a very open-minded person.

Emotional Freedom Technique (Tapping)

EFT (Emotional Freedom Technique) is a universal healing aid that rebalances the body's energy system with respect to unresolved emotional issues. Energy meridians that run through our body can be blocked or disrupted by unresolved emotional issues, thereby compromising our natural healing potential. Realigning the energy meridians while focusing on an unresolved emotional issue can often provide increased personal peace and relief from many physical symptoms.

Although based on the principles of acupuncture, EFT has simplified the realignment process by gently tapping on key meridian points on the head, torso and hands. Traditional acupuncture needles are not necessary in this process, and it can be learned and applied by anyone.

Okay, that's the complicated definition. In simple terms, you tap your fingers on certain areas of your body, while speaking phrases and affirmations to yourself, in an attempt to clear a fear, phobia, or even some physical problem.

I am not a professional at this method, and only mention it here because I've tried it (with great skepticism), and actually had excellent results. It only takes a few minutes to learn, and is very easy. It is goofy! Even practitioners agree...You look very goofy when doing it. So just be prepared if you try it.

Anyway, I did have positive results using it. You basically affirm a situation you want to change, and while saying the affirmation repeatedly, you tap on specific meridian points on the body, supposedly releasing the negative energy while tapping. Let's say you feel fear about something. So while you are tapping on the meridian points, you affirm to yourself your feeling fearful by saying repeatedly "I am afraid". This supposedly alleviates the fear you're feeling.

If you're interested, I have a link you can go to:

Youtube EFT Tapping

There is so much information on the internet on EFT your head may spin. But I want you to know that this really weird method worked for me. However, I don't think it was the actual tapping that worked. I think it was the repetitive affirmations that helped me. I'm really a big proponent of affirmations.

In fact, I've studied numerous successful people for years, and almost all of them use affirmations in their lives. It's a simple, effective method of getting into a state you really desire to be in, and works quite quickly.

The difference between affirming and using EFT tapping is the movement of your body.

I say; if you're struggling with resistance and blocks, take a look at this. Like I said, I was (pleasantly) surprised after trying it, and practicing it a bit. It may be what you're looking for.

There are a lot of practitioners out there now, so I won't name names. I am not promoting anyone's services in this book, just guiding you as best I can to help you reach your goals.

So take a look.

Youtube EFT Tapping

Meditation

I'll touch on meditation briefly. Meditation is one of the best ways to clear your mind and body of blocks, resistance, and any other kinds of negativity. When done correctly, and regularly, it can bring feelings of peace and happiness: A feeling of oneness with the Universe.

Yes, I meditate every single day, and have done so for about 8 years. There is no doubt in my mind that it has helped me find great inner-peace. I'm relaxed. I'm calm. I have clarity.

The best part about meditation, if it is something you want to venture into, is that I have already shown you how to enter a meditative state. If you look in the Imagination/Visualization chapter, the same way you relax for visualization is pretty much the same way you meditate.

Put yourself in a relaxed position. Sitting is preferred, but I've known many people who meditate lying down (just don't fall asleep). Close your eyes. Breathe deeply. Relax the muscles in your body from head to toe. Count backwards from 10 to 1. For 15-30 minutes, concentrate on your breathing, or say one single mantra (like "I am one with the Universe). Keep the mind otherwise clear. If thoughts enter the mind, just release them.

That's it. And just practice, practice, practice.

There are also programs you can buy to help put you in a meditative state. This entails using headphones and either CD's or MP3 downloads that use binaural beats to put your brain into certain brainwave frequencies. Regular meditation is thought to do the same thing. I can tell you through personal experience that some of the binaural beats programs on the market are quite good. To add to that, learning standard meditation takes a very long time to master, while the binaural beats programs are very quick and easy to use.

I have used both Brain Sync and the Centerpointe Holosync program. Both are excellent. Brain Sync offers numerous meditation CD's and MP3 downloads at a very inexpensive price. Centerpointe's Holosync is what I would call a dedicated meditation program. You will devote years to the program, going in to deeper and deeper meditations as time passes. The program is not cheap, so you should be truly interested in making a deep commitment to meditating for an hour daily with Holosync. There are other programs on the market, but I've had enough success using these two companies that I can say with utmost confidence; one of them can fill your needs if you decide to meditate using binaural beats.

The bottom line; meditating can definitely increase your power to create what you want in your life. It really opens your mind to a wonderful inner-peace, which helps remove resistance. I highly recommend it!

Goals and Goal Setting
Your Purpose

I've lumped goals, setting your goals, and purpose into one, small briefing. I'll explain why as I go along.

I have read countless writings on goals and goal setting. I've read you should have as many goals as possible, thousands if you can think of that many. I've also read you're better off having a few goals...short term, intermediate term, and long term. Financial, health, relationships, etc.

The problem is this…

In all the readings I've done from the "experts" on goal setting, there tends to be a differing of opinions. Some say we should set goals outrageously high, while others say to set them at believable levels. Which method works best? Which method is the right one?

I have had mixed results with both. So what I've done is this...I've set intermediate term goals for myself, but I don't call them goals. I call them Desires and Intentions.

Are goals really any different from your desires? I don't think so. Put your goals down on paper, reflect upon them, and figure out a way to make them happen. Take action when necessary. See the chapter on Desire. It's the same.

So as far as goals and goal setting goes...Do the same as you'd do for your desires.

Make a list of how you want your life to be. What you want in your life. Who you want in your life. Then put a time frame you would like to achieve these desires. One year, three years, ten years, twenty years. Have some clarity. Don't make yourself crazy.

Goal setting tends to stress people out. They want to have so much in their lives, but can't grasp how to get there. If you're one of these types, where goal setting makes you nuts, just relax. I would make some simple, but clear, short to intermediate term goals...But have a few really powerful desires. And put your focus there. Once you deliberately start manifesting things in your life, your Belief levels go through the roof! That's the best time for goal setting.

The funny thing about goals is that they always change. As you achieve goals, or don't quite make it, the next goals in your mind are always different. Your goals are always changing so don't get crazy over this.

Set some goals (desires), and go for it. Be flexible along the way. Feel good about it.

As far as your purpose...I've seen a bit of an *'explosion'* lately on what a person's purpose is or should be. Why are you here? What is your specific purpose on earth?

Many LOA practitioners are pushing this lately. We all have a special purpose.

Don't get me wrong, I think everyone has special gifts and talents. But I think your purpose for being here is simple.

JOY!

How can you narrow down a specific purpose for someone? Look at Michael Jordan. Many have said his purpose was to play basketball. That is ridiculous!

His ultimate talent was being a great basketball player. He was amazing! But he also inspired millions of people. He's become a business entrepreneur; his name has actually provided thousands of jobs around the world. He has brought JOY to millions. Look beyond the basketball...It's bigger than that.

Your purpose is to be as joyful and happy as possible. Find and use your talents, and share them with the world.

Your purpose is Joy!

Love

Since I've told you your secret purpose is joy (just kidding), let's move to the grand finale of the whole reason for being…

Love. What is love?

Love is kindness. Love is appreciation. Love is affection. Love is abundance. Love encompasses every positive emotion you can think of. It encompasses joy. It encompasses gratitude.

Love conquers all.

I guess I could go on and on and on. Your purpose is Joy. Your reason for being here is Love. In fact, I have heard many of the older practitioners call the Law of Attraction the Law of Love. What would our lives be like without it? Can you imagine your own life without some form of love in it?

You see, you can't actually imagine what life could be like without love; without human kindness and compassion. If you're currently not feeling it, try to open yourself up to love. Love changes your life.

Love makes us who we are.

Love helps us through tough times.

Love makes us better.

Love is all that is.

You are here to love, and be loved. It is the ultimate achievement.

Love yourself and love all of humanity. The creator of all that is loves you, and everyone else.

Be loving and you will receive love.

Law of Attraction Cheat Sheet

Questions to Ask Yourself before Visualizing

1. How do I feel? Positive or Negative?
2. How am I 'Being'? How am I vibrating?
3. How strong is my desire?
4. Do I BELIEVE it's possible?
5. Does my desire make me feel really good (Burning Desire)?
6. Is my desire for the highest good of all concerned?
7. How can I feel good right now?

****

Visualization

1. Write down your desire
2. Relax (eyes closed)
3. Visualize (Imagine your desire has already happened)
4. Really FEEL IT!
5. Positive Statement of your Intention
6. Closing Statement

****

How to Feel Great
Physiology, Affirmations, Questions

1. Practice feeling (looking) good in front of a mirror. Smile!
2. Do you look happy?
3. Use physiology techniques. (Get pumped up)
4. Listen to your favorite music.
5. Exercise
6. Yell and Scream (Gets the heart pumping)
7. Speak to yourself with kindness, respect, and love.
8. Affirm positive statements nonstop until state changes.
9. Use empowering questions to get positive, justified responses from your mind.
10. Do whatever it takes to FEEL GOOD!!

* If you feel really good, you will manifest more goodness in to your life! *

Final Note

On the next page is a small list of resources. Books, videos, authors...Which you MAY feel the need to look into.

They are all excellent. I don't think they are completely necessary, but you may find them inspirational. I say unnecessary because you already have everything you need.

Follow *'this'* book's instructions, mix in the ingredients of the LOA "cookbook", and be persistent. Never, Ever, Give up!

The first 3 resources I would highly recommend...Especially "Creative Visualization". I used these 3 books more than anything else on my way to success and happiness, and eventually realized they were all I needed. Even though I feel that if you just follow the instructions in this book is all you need – Adding the top 3 books will truly help you.

The rest of the resources are listed in order of preference.

Now go for it!

Follow the instructions. Become the person you truly desire to be. If I can do it, I know you can also.

My deepest desire:

I desire that my written words serve you well. That this book contributes to your life in ways that are far beyond my imagination and yours as well.

I wish you all the best! You deserve it!

Resources

My Top 3 Books

Think and Grow Rich by Napoleon Hill
There have been more millionaires who have made their fortunes as a result of this book than any other in print today.

The Science of Getting Rich by Wallace D. Wattles
The original and best guide to manifesting wealth through the Law of Attraction. A major inspiration for Rhonda Byrne's bestselling book "The Secret".
Also:
http://www.scienceofgettingrich.net/

Creative Visualization by Shakti Gawain
A simple yet powerful guide on using your imagination to manifest your desires.
Also:
http://www.shaktigawain.com/

Other Great Resources

Personal Power by Anthony Robbins (CD's)
One of the most popular and influential personal achievement programs of all time.
Also:
Awaken the Giant Within (Book)
Unlimited Power (Book)
http://www.tonyrobbins.com/

The Master Key System by Charles F. Haanel
Written approximately the same time as "The Science of Getting Rich". Also said to have influenced Rhonda Byrne's "The Secret". Supposedly influenced Bill Gates to leave college to found Microsoft.

Ask and It Is Given – Learning to Manifest Your Desires by Jerry and Esther Hicks (as Abraham)
Esther Hicks, who channels a non-physical collective of entities calling themselves Abraham, teaches how to manifest your desires.
Also:
Many books, CD's, videos
www.abraham-hicks.com

The Secret by Rhonda Byrne
This book, and the movie of the same title, started a mass awakening to the Law of Attraction concepts.
Also:
The Magic (book)
http://thesecret.tv/index.html

A Happy Pocket Full of Money by David Cameron Gikandi
A very interesting, and useful perspective on creating what you desire. The author was a consultant to the making of the movie "The Secret".

Real Magic: Creating Miracles in Everyday Life by Dr. Wayne Dyer
A bit more on the spiritual side, Dr. Dyer reveals ways to achieve desired changes to your life.
Also:
Numerous books, CD's, and seminars
http://www.drwaynedyer.com/

The Success Principles: How to Get from Where You Are to Where you Want to Be by Jack Canfield and Janet Switzer
This book was written highlighting 64 principles used by successful men and women throughout history. Canfield co-wrote the bestseller "Chicken Soup for The Soul".
Also:
Books, CD's, video's
http://jackcanfield.com/

7 Strategies for Wealth and Happiness by Jim Rohn
Wealth strategy book written by one of the top motivational speakers in the field.
Also:
Books, CD's
http://www.jimrohn.com/home

You Can Heal Your Life by Louise Hay
The timeless message of the book is that we are each responsible for our own reality and "dis-ease."
Louise Hay is founder and chairman of Hay House, Inc. which disseminates books, CD's, DVD's, and other products that contribute to the healing of the planet.
Also:
http://www.hayhouse.com/

One Last Important Thing

If you've enjoyed this book, please consider leaving a review at the retailer that you purchased this book. It's the ultimate form of flattery for an author.
I love hearing from you, and it's a great way for other readers to discover new books!

Eksanto.com
eksanto1966@gmail.com

Look for me on Facebook: How I Made Over $1 Million Using the Law of Attraction

Find me on Twitter:
https://twitter.com/EKSanto1966

Printed in Great Britain
by Amazon